SCOTLAND
SLANG

★ ★ ★ ★ ★ ★ ★ ★ ★ ★ ★ ★

WORDS & PHRASES

Immerse yourself in the lively realm of Scottish slang with this essential companion. It is ideal for travelers, language enthusiasts, or those intrigued by Scottish culture.

•Uncover popular Scottish terms and phrases, demystified through straightforward definitions.

•Benefit from a pronunciation key accompanying each slang expression

•Delve into practical examples showcasing the usage of these colorful terms in everyday discourse.

•Encounter amusing and time-honored Scottish idioms and phrases on your linguistic journey.

Contents

Scottish Slang Pronunciation Tips

A - The letter "A" is pronounced like the "ay" in the word "day."

B - The letter "B" is pronounced like the word "bee," as in the insect.

C - Letter C is pronounced like 'see,' as in the word 'to see something.'

D - Pronounced like "dee," as in the letter "D."

E - The letter E is pronounced like 'ee,' as in the word 'see.'

F - Pronounced like 'eff,' as in the English letter F.

G - Pronounced like "gee," as in "gee whiz" (an expression of surprise).

H - Pronounced like "aitch," with the 'h' sound at the beginning.

I - Pronounced like "eye," as in "I see you."

J - Pronounced like "jay," as in a blue jay bird.

K - Say "kay," as in "ok."

L - Say "ell," as the name of the letter.

M - Say "em," as the name of the letter.

N - Say "en," as the name of the letter.

O - Say "oh," as in "oh no."

P - Say "pee," as in the act of urination.

Q - Say "queue," like a line of waiting people.

R - The letter R is pronounced like 'ar,' with a slight roll of the 'r.'

S - Spoken in ess as in the letter "S."

T - Spoken in tee as in the letter "T."

U - Pronounced you with a slight "y" sound at the beginning.

V - The letter V has the same pronunciation as it does.

W- It is pronounced as "double you" because of the letter's shape.

X- Spoken like "ex" as in "exit."

Y- Like "why" as in questioning.

Z- The pronunciation for the letter Z is 'zee' if the American accent

is used, and for the British accent, it is 'zed'.

Aboot

- Pronunciation:

Uh-boot

- Meaning:

About or Around

- Example of use:

"Let's talk aboot the plans for the weekend."

Ae

- Pronunciation:

Ay

- Meaning:

One

- Example of use:

"I'll have ae coffee, please."

Aff

- Pronunciation:

Aff

- Meaning:

Off

- Example of use:

"She's aff to a meeting."

Ah Wisnae

- Pronunciation:

Ah wiz-nay

- Meaning:

I Wasn't

- Example of use:

"Ah wisnae aware of the changes."

Ah Wiz Like

- Pronunciation:

Ah wiz lyke

- Meaning:

I Said / I Was Like

- Example of use:

"Ah wiz like, 'Let's go to the beach!'"

Ah'm No

- Pronunciation:

Ahm noh

- Meaning:

I'm Not

- Example of use:

"Ah'm no going to the party tonight."

Ah'm Ur

- Pronunciation:

Ahm ur

- Meaning:

I Am / I'm Your

- Example of use:

"Ah'm ur best friend."

Auld

- Pronunciation:

Awld

- Meaning:

Old

- Example of use:

"That's an auld book."

Awfy

- Pronunciation:

Aw-fee

- Meaning:

Awfully or Extremely

- Example of use:

"It's an awfy long journey."

Awright

- Pronunciation:

Aw-right

- Meaning:

Alright

- Example of use:

"How are you? Awright?"

Aye

- Pronunciation:

Ay

- Meaning:

Yes

- Example of use:

"Aye, I'll be there on time."

Aabody

- Pronunciation:

A-buh-dee

- Meaning:

Everybody or Everyone

- Example of use:

"Aabody is invited to the party."

Baccy

• Pronunciation:

Bak-ee

• Meaning:

Tobacco

• Example of use:

"Do you have any baccy for my pipe?"

Baffies

• Pronunciation:

Baf-ees

• Meaning:

Sippers

• Example of use:

"I need to find my baffies before bed."

Bairn

• Pronunciation:

Bern

• Meaning:

Child

• Example of use:

"The bairn is having a nap."

Baltic

- Pronunciation:

Bal-tik

- Meaning:

Freezing Cold

- Example of use:

"It's baltic outside, better wrap up warm."

Bampot

- Pronunciation:

Bam-pot

- Meaning:

a Fool or Annoying

- Example of use:

"Don't be such a bampot, you're making a fool of yourself."

Barkit

- Pronunciation:

Bar-kit

- Meaning:

Unclean

- Example of use:

"The kitchen is barkit, it needs a good clean."

Barry

- Pronunciation:

Bar-ee

- Meaning:

Brilliant

- Example of use:

"That concert was barry, I had a great time."

Bawbag

- Pronunciation:

Bah-bag

- Meaning:

An insult meaning "scrotum" or "jerk"

- Example of use:

"He's being such a bawbag today, can't stand him."

Belter

- Pronunciation:

Bel-ter

- Meaning:

Great, Excellent, It's a Statement of Positive Opinion

- Example of use:

"That film was an absolute belter, I highly recommend it."

Ben

- Pronunciation:

Ben

- Meaning:

an Interior Room Within a House or Cottage

- Example of use:

"Let's have a chat in the ben."

Bide

- Pronunciation:

Byde

- Meaning:

Stay or to Linger

- Example of use:

"I'll bide here until you're ready to go."

Big man / Big yin

- Pronunciation:

Big man / big yin

- Meaning:

Term of Address for a Man

- Example of use:

"Hey, big man, how's it going?"

Bit

·Pronunciation:

Bit

·Meaning:

Someone's Residence

·Example of use:

"I'm heading to his bit for a cup of tea."

Bits

·Pronunciation:

Bitz

·Meaning:

Footwear Worn on Construction Sites

·Example of use:

"Make sure you wear your bits on the construction site."

Bizzo

·Pronunciation:

Biz-o

·Meaning:

Business

·Example of use:

"He's always busy with his bizzo."

Blether

- Pronunciation:

Bleth-er

- Meaning:

Talk Too Much

- Example of use:

"She can blether for hours about anything."

Boak

- Pronunciation:

Boke

- Meaning:

to Vomit

- Example of use:

"The smell of that fish made him boak."

Bonnie

- Pronunciation:

Bon-ee

- Meaning:

Beautiful or Attractive

- Example of use:

"She looked bonnie in her new dress."

Bosie

- Pronunciation:

Bo-see

- Meaning:

Cuddle

- Example of use:

"Can I have a bosie before you go?"

Bowfin

- Pronunciation:

Bow-fin

- Meaning:

Foul Smelling or Tasting/unpalatable

- Example of use:

"The milk was bowfin, I had to throw it out."

Brae

- Pronunciation:

Bray

- Meaning:

Crest of a Hill

- Example of use:

"Let's hike to the brae and enjoy the view."

Brammer

- Pronunciation:

Bram-er

- Meaning:

Something Exceptional or Outstanding

- Example of use:

"That performance was a real brammer!"

Braw

- Pronunciation:

Braw

- Meaning:

Good or Excellent

- Example of use:

"This tea is braw, thank you."

Breeks

- Pronunciation:

Breeks

- Meaning:

Trousers

- Example of use:

"He wore his best breeks to the party."

Broon

- Pronunciation:

Broon

- Meaning:

Brown

- Example of use:

"She painted the door broon."

Bunker

- Pronunciation:

Bunk-er

- Meaning:

Table Top

- Example of use:

"She placed the vase on the bunker."

Burd

- Pronunciation:

Buh-rd

- Meaning:

a Young Lady

- Example of use:

"He's taking his burd out for dinner."

Burn

- Pronunciation:

Bern

- Meaning:

a Small River, Stream, or Rivulet

- Example of use:

"Let's have a picnic by the burn."

Cannae

- Pronunciation:

Can-ay

- Meaning:

Cannot

- Example of use:

"I cannae make it to the party tonight."

Canny

- Pronunciation:

Can-ee

- Meaning:

Smart, Clever or Cunning / Careful

- Example of use:

"She's a canny lass, always thinking ahead."

Cauld / Chankin

- Pronunciation:

Cawld / Chan-kin

- Meaning:

Very Cold

- Example of use:

"It's cauld outside, don't forget your jacket."

Chook / Chookie

- Pronunciation:

Chook / Choo-kee

- Meaning:

Chick, a Chicken

- Example of use:

"Let's have some chook for dinner."

Choon

- Pronunciation:

Choon

- Meaning:

a Favorite Track or Song

- Example of use:

"That's my choon! Turn it up!"

Chuffed

- Pronunciation:

Chuff-ed

- Meaning:

Pleased

- Example of use:

"She was chuffed with her exam results."

Chum

- Pronunciation:

Chum

- Meaning:

to Accompany Someone

- Example of use:

"Can you chum me to the shops?"

Claes

- Pronunciation:

Clays

- Meaning:

Clothes

- Example of use:

"I need to buy some new claes for the party."

Clatty

- Pronunciation:

Clat-ee

- Meaning:

Dirty or Messy

- Example of use:

"Her room is clatty, she should clean it up."

Clipe

- Pronunciation:

Clyp

- Meaning:

Someone Who Tells on You "grass" "a Tell Tale"

- Example of use:

"Don't be a clipe and tell on your friends."

Close

- Pronunciation:

Cloze

- Meaning:

Alleyway or Narrow Passage

- Example of use:

"He lives in the close down the road."

Cludgie

- Pronunciation:

Klud-jee

- Meaning:

Toilet

- Example of use:

"Where's the cludgie in this place?"

Coo

- Pronunciation:

Koo

- Meaning:

Cow

- Example of use:

"The coo is grazing in the field."

Cooncil Juice

- Pronunciation:

Coon-sil Joo-iss

- Meaning:

Tap Water

- Example of use:

"I'll just have some cooncil juice, please."

Cowk

- Pronunciation:

  Cawk

- Meaning:

  Feel Nauseated

- Example of use:

  "That smell makes me cowk."

Cowp

- Pronunciation:

  Coup

- Meaning:

  to Knock Over. Also, a Skip or Landfill

- Example of use:

  "Don't cowp that glass over!"

Crabbit

- Pronunciation:

  Crab-it

- Meaning:

  Bad-tempered or Grumpy

- Example of use:

  "He's always crabbit in the mornings."

Craic / Crack

- Pronunciation:

Crak

- Meaning:

a Clever or Humorous Remark, a Wisecrack

- Example of use:

"That was a good craic at the party last night."

Crivens

- Pronunciation:

Kriv-ens

- Meaning:

an Expression of Amazement

- Example of use:

"Crivens, I can't believe you did that!"

Cuddy

- Pronunciation:

Kud-ee

- Meaning:

Horse

- Example of use:

"Let's go for a ride on the cuddy."

Cummoan

- Pronunciation:

Kum-moan

- Meaning:

Let's Go

- Example of use:

"Cummoan, we're going to be late!"

Da

- Pronunciation:

Dah

- Meaning:

Father

- Example of use:

"My da is picking me up from school today."

Dae

- Pronunciation:

Day

- Meaning:

Do

- Example of use:

"Whit dae ye dae fur a living?"

Dafty

- Pronunciation:

Dahf-tee

- Meaning:

Silly or Foolish

- Example of use:

"Stop being a dafty and listen to me."

Dander / Daunner

- Pronunciation:

Dan-der / Dan-er

- Meaning:

a Walk or a Stroll

- Example of use:

"Let's go for a dander along the beach."

Deh

- Pronunciation:

Deh

- Meaning:

Don't

- Example of use:

"Deh be late for the meeting."

Deid

- Pronunciation:

Deed

- Meaning:

Dead

- Example of use:

"The battery is deid, I need to charge it."

Di

- Pronunciation:

Dye

- Meaning:

Grandad

- Example of use:

"Di tells the best stories."

Didnae

- Pronunciation:

Did-nay

- Meaning:

Didn't

- Example of use:

"I didnae have time to finish my homework."

Div

- Pronunciation:

Div

- Meaning:

Idiot

- Example of use:

"He's acting like a total div today."

Doo

- Pronunciation:

Doo

- Meaning:

a Pigeon

- Example of use:

"Look at that doo perched on the fence."

Doon

- Pronunciation:

Doon

- Meaning:

Down

- Example of use:

"Head on doon to the shop and get some milk."

Doric

- Pronunciation:

Door-ik

- Meaning:

Scots Dialect Spoken in the North East of Scotland

- Example of use:

"She speaks in Doric when she's with her family."

Dreich

- Pronunciation:

Dreich

- Meaning:

Dull or Gloomy

- Example of use:

"It's a dreich day outside, best stay indoors."

Drookit

- Pronunciation:

Drook-it

- Meaning:

Soaked or Drenched

- Example of use:

"I got caught in the rain and now I'm drookit."

Dug

- Pronunciation:

Dug

- Meaning:

Dog

- Example of use:

"His dug is always by his side."

Dunderheid

- Pronunciation:

Dun-der-hed

- Meaning:

Idiot

- Example of use:

"He's a right dunderheid for forgetting his keys again."

Dunno / Dinnae Ken

- Pronunciation:

Dun-no / Din-ay ken

- Meaning:

I Don't Know

- Example of use:

"Sorry, I dunno where I left my phone."

Dunt

- Pronunciation:

Dunt

- Meaning:

Nudge or Hard Blow

- Example of use:

"He gave me a dunt on the shoulder to get my attention."

Efter

- Pronunciation:

Eft-er

- Meaning:

After

- Example of use:

"I'll meet you efter work for a drink."

Fa

- Pronunciation:

Fah

- Meaning:

to Fall, to Happen to One, Fall, Befall

- Example of use:

"I hope nothing bad fa's to you on your trip."

Fae

- Pronunciation:

Fay

- Meaning:

From

- Example of use:

"I'm fae Glasgow."

Faimly

- Pronunciation:

Fam-lee

- Meaning:

Family

- Example of use:

"She's spending time with her faimly this weekend."

Faither

- Pronunciation:

Fay-ther

- Meaning:

Father

- Example of use:

"My faither taught me how to fish."

Fankle

- Pronunciation:

Fan-kul

- Meaning:

to Become Entangled or Ensnared

- Example of use:

"I fankled the wires together by mistake."

Fash

- Pronunciation:

Fash

- Meaning:

Bother or Trouble

- Example of use:

"Don't fash yourself over it, it's not a big deal."

Feart

- Pronunciation:

Feert

- Meaning:

Afraid

- Example of use:

"He's feart of spiders."

Fearthainn

- Pronunciation:

Feer-han

- Meaning:

Heavy Rain

- Example of use:

"It's pouring out there, must be fearthainn."

Feartie

- Pronunciation:

Feer-tee

- Meaning:

Coward

- Example of use:

"Don't be a feartie, face your fears."

Fit Like?

- Pronunciation:

Fit Like

- Meaning:

a Way of Asking "How Are You?"

- Example of use:

"Fit like? How's it going?"

Fit You

- Pronunciation:

Fit Yoo

- Meaning:

What You

- Example of use:

"Fit you dain the day?"

Fitba

- Pronunciation:

Fit-ba

- Meaning:

Football

- Example of use:

"Let's head to the park and play some fitba."

Flair

- Pronunciation:

Flair

- Meaning:

Floor

- Example of use:

"The cat's always sitting on the flair."

Forby

- Pronunciation:

For-bye

- Meaning:

in Addition

- Example of use:

"I'll have a coffee and a cake forby."

Fower

- Pronunciation:

Fower

- Meaning:

Four

- Example of use:

"There are fower chairs at the table."

Fowk

- Pronunciation:

"fok" rhyming with "poke."

- Meaning:

Folk

- Example of use:

"The local fowk are friendly around here."

Frae

•Pronunciation:

"Fray" (rhymes with "say")

•Meaning:

From

•Example of use:

"I'm frae Edinburgh."

Frei

•Pronunciation:

Fray

•Meaning:

Friend

•Example of use:

"He's been a good frei for years."

Fush

•Pronunciation:

Fish

•Meaning:

Fish

•Example of use:

"I fancy some fush and chips for dinner."

Gae

- Pronunciation:

Gay

- Meaning:

Go

- Example of use:

"Let's gae and see what's happening."

Gaff

- Pronunciation:

Gaff

- Meaning:

House

- Example of use:

"I'm heading back to the gaff, see you later."

Gallus

- Pronunciation:

Gal-lus

- Meaning:

Confident or Stylish

- Example of use:

"She walked in with a gallus attitude."

Ginger

- Pronunciation:

Jin-jer

- Meaning:

Fizzy Drink

- Example of use:

"Pass me a can of ginger."

Girdle

- Pronunciation:

Gur-dul

- Meaning:

Griddle

- Example of use:

"The scones are cooking on the girdle."

Girn

- Pronunciation:

Girn

- Meaning:

Grumble or Discontent

- Example of use:

"Stop yer girnin' and get on with it."

Glaikit

- Pronunciation:

Glake-it

- Meaning:

Silly

- Example of use:

"He's always pulling glaikit faces."

Glaswegian

- Pronunciation:

Glas-wee-jan

- Meaning:

a Person From Glasgow

- Example of use:

"She's a proud Glaswegian."

Glaur

- Pronunciation:

Glor

- Meaning:

Muck or Mire

- Example of use:

"Don't step in the glaur, it's muddy."

Glen

- Pronunciation:

    Glen

- Meaning:

    Valley

- Example of use:

    "The river flows through the glen."

Glescae

- Pronunciation:

    Gless-kay

- Meaning:

    Glasgow

- Example of use:

    "I'm heading to Glescae for the weekend."

Gloaming

- Pronunciation:

    Glow-ming

- Meaning:

    Twilight

- Example of use:

    "The sky was beautiful in the gloaming."

Goun

- Pronunciation:

Goon

- Meaning:

a Night-shirt

- Example of use:

"She put on her goun and settled in for the night."

Gowk

- Pronunciation:

Gowk

- Meaning:

a Foolish Person

- Example of use:

"Don't be such a gowk, think before you speak."

Greet

- Pronunciation:

Greet

- Meaning:

a Complaining Person

- Example of use:

"She's always a greet about the weather."

Greetin

- Pronunciation:

  Greet-in

- Meaning:

  Crying or Weeping

- Example of use:

  "He was greetin' after watching that sad movie."

Guid Day

- Pronunciation:

  Gwid Day

- Meaning:

  Good Day

- Example of use:

  "Guid day to you, sir!"

Gutties

- Pronunciation:

  Gut-tees

- Meaning:

  Shoes or Plimsoles

- Example of use:

  "I need to buy a new pair of gutties for gym class."

Hae

- Pronunciation:

    "Hay" (rhymes with "say")

- Meaning:

    Have

- Example of use:

    "I hae a meeting at 3 o'clock."

Hame

- Pronunciation:

    "Hame" (rhymes with "same")

- Meaning:

    Home

- Example of use:

    "Let's head hame for dinner."

Haud

- Pronunciation:

    "Hawd" (rhymes with "awed")

- Meaning:

    Hold

- Example of use:

    "Haud on a minute, I'm coming!"

Hauf

- Pronunciation:

  "Haff" (rhymes with "staff")

- Meaning:

  Half

- Example of use:

  "I'll have hauf a pint, please."

Heid

- Pronunciation:

  "Heed" (rhymes with "seed")

- Meaning:

  Head

- Example of use:

  "I've got a headache in ma heid."

Hen

- Pronunciation:

  Hen

- Meaning:

  Darling or Dear

- Example of use:

  "Thanks, hen, you've been a great help."

Hiya! / Hey Up

- Pronunciation:

Hi-ya! / Hay-up

- Meaning:

Hello

- Example of use:

"Hiya, how are ye?"

Hoachin'

- Pronunciation:

Hoach-in

- Meaning:

Very Busy

- Example of use:

"The place was hoachin' with folk last night."

Hogmanay

- Pronunciation:

Hog-ma-nay

- Meaning:

New Year's Eve

- Example of use:

"Are ye comin' tae the Hogmanay party?"

Hoose

- Pronunciation:

Hoose

- Meaning:

House

- Example of use:

"I'm cleanin' the hoose today."

Howsit?

- Pronunciation:

Howz-it?

- Meaning:

How Are You?

- Example of use:

"Howsit gaun the day?"

How's It Gaun?

- Pronunciation:

Howz-it Gone?

- Meaning:

How Are You Doing?

- Example of use:

"How's it gaun, pal?"

Hullo

- Pronunciation:

Hull-o

- Meaning:

Hello

- Example of use:

"Hullo there, nice to see ye!"

Ilka

- Pronunciation:

Il-ka

- Meaning:

Every

- Example of use:

"Ilka Thursday, we go for a walk."

Intae

- Pronunciation:

In-tay

- Meaning:

Into

- Example of use:

"Let's go intae town for a bit."

Jalouse

- Pronunciation:

Ja-looz

- Meaning:

to Suspect or Guess

- Example of use:

"I jalouse he's nae comin'."

Jimmy

- Pronunciation:

Jim-mee

- Meaning:

a Common Term of Address to a Man, Often a Stranger

- Example of use:

"Excuse me, Jimmy, d'ye ken the way to the station?"

Jings!

- Pronunciation:

"jings!" (with a short "i" sound)

- Meaning:

an Exclamation or to Express Surprise

- Example of use:

"Jings, I cannae believe it!"

Jist

- Pronunciation:

Jist

- Meaning:

Just

- Example of use:

"I'll be back in a minute, jist wait here."

Keek

- Pronunciation:

"keek" (with a short "e" sound)

- Meaning:

Stealthily Look

- Example of use:

"Let's keek around the corner and see what they're up to."

Ken

- Pronunciation:

"ken" (with a short "e" sound)

- Meaning:

You Know?

- Example of use:

"It's a braw day, ken?"

Lad

• Pronunciation:

Lad

• Meaning:

Man or Youth

• Example of use:

"That lad over there is a good football player."

Laich

• Pronunciation:

Lay-ch

• Meaning:

Lowly

• Example of use:

"He comes from a laich background."

Laldie

• Pronunciation:

Lal-dee

• Meaning:

Great Enthusiasm or Energy

• Example of use:

"She danced with laldie at the party."

Lang

- Pronunciation:

Lang

- Meaning:

Long

- Example of use:

"It's been a lang day at work."

Lassie

- Pronunciation:

Lass-ee

- Meaning:

A Young woman or girl, sometimes informally
referred to as "sweetheart."

- Example of use:

"The lassie at the shop was very helpful."

Lavvy

- Pronunciation:

Lav-ee

- Meaning:

Toilet

- Example of use:

"Excuse me, where's the lavvy?"

Loch

- Pronunciation:

    "loch" (with a long "o" sound)

- Meaning:

    Lake

- Example of use:

    "Let's go for a swim in the loch."

Loon

- Pronunciation:

    "loon" (with a long "oo" sound)

- Meaning:

    Boy or Young Man

- Example of use:

    "The loon fixed my bike for me."

Loup

- Pronunciation:

    Loop

- Meaning:

    Leap

- Example of use:

    "She took a loup over the fence."

Loupin

- Pronunciation:

Loop-in

- Meaning:

Extremely Painful

- Example of use:

"My knee is loupin after that fall."

Lugs

- Pronunciation:

lugz

- Meaning:

Ears

- Example of use:

"He whispered in my lugs."

Lum

- Pronunciation:

Lum

- Meaning:

Chimney

- Example of use:

"The lum was smoking this morning."

Ma

- Pronunciation:

Ma

- Meaning:

My

- Example of use:

"Ma phone is ringing."

Mair

- Pronunciation:

Mare

- Meaning:

More

- Example of use:

"Can I have mair sugar in my tea, please?"

Maist

- Pronunciation:

Mast

- Meaning:

Most

- Example of use:

"He's the maist talented musician in the band."

Makar

- Pronunciation:

  MAH-kur

- Meaning:

  Poet

- Example of use:

  "My dad is famous Poet."

Manky

- Pronunciation:

  Mang-kee

- Meaning:

  Dirty or Gross

- Example of use:

  "That river is manky, don't swim in it."

Mate

- Pronunciation:

  Mate

- Meaning:

  Friend

- Example of use:

  "John's been my mate since we were kids."

Maun

- Pronunciation:

Mawn

- Meaning:

Must

- Example of use:

"Ye maun be joking!"

Maw / Mither

- Pronunciation:

Maw/Mith-er

- Meaning:

Mother

- Example of use:

"I'm going to visit my maw this weekend."

Merrit

- Pronunciation:

Mer-it

- Meaning:

Married

- Example of use:

"They got merrit last summer."

Messages

· Pronunciation:

Mess-a-jes

· Meaning:

Groceries or Shopping

· Example of use:

"I need to pick up the messages on the way home."

Micht

· Pronunciation:

Mikht

· Meaning:

Might

· Example of use:

"I micht be a bit late for dinner."

Michty!

· Pronunciation:

Mikht-ee

· Meaning:

Wow! Or Exclamation of Surprise

· Example of use:

"Michty, that was a close call!"

Midden

- Pronunciation:

    Mid-den

- Meaning:

    Refuse Heap

- Example of use:

    "The old car was left in the midden."

Mince

- Pronunciation:

    Mins

- Meaning:

    Nonsense

- Example of use:

    "Don't talk mince, tell me the truth."

Mind

- Pronunciation:

    Mind

- Meaning:

    Remember

- Example of use:

    "Mind to pick up some milk on your way home."

Mingin

- Pronunciation:

Ming-in

- Meaning:

Stinking or Disgusting

- Example of use:

"The bins are mingin today."

Minted

- Pronunciation:

Min-ted

- Meaning:

Rich or Wealthy

- Example of use:

"He's absolutely minted after winning the lottery."

Mon

- Pronunciation:

Mon

- Meaning:

Man

- Example of use:

"Mon, let's go watch the game together."

Mony

· Pronunciation:

Mo-nee

· Meaning:

Many

· Example of use:

"There are mony reasons to visit Scotland."

Moose

· Pronunciation:

Moos

· Meaning:

Mouse

· Example of use:

"There's a moose in the kitchen!"

Mooth

· Pronunciation:

Mooth

· Meaning:

Mouth

· Example of use:

"Shut your mooth and listen for a minute."

Morra

- Pronunciation:

Mor-ra

- Meaning:

Tomorrow

- Example of use:

"I'll see you at the pub morra."

Muckle

- Pronunciation:

Muk-kle

- Meaning:

Large or Big or Much

- Example of use:

"That's a muckle fish you caught."

Muir

- Pronunciation:

Moor

- Meaning:

Moor or Moorland

- Example of use:

"Let's take a walk on the muir this weekend."

Nae Bother

- Pronunciation:

Nay Bother

- Meaning:

No Problem

- Example of use:

"Thanks for helping out, nae bother."

Nae / Naw

- Pronunciation:

Nay / Naw

- Meaning:

No or Not

- Example of use:

"Nae way I'm going out in this weather."

Neeps

- Pronunciation:

Neeps

- Meaning:

Turnips

- Example of use:

"Neeps are a traditional Scottish dish."

Neuk

- Pronunciation:

  Neeps

- Meaning:

  Nook or Corner

- Example of use:

  "She found a cozy neuk to read her book."

Ne'er

- Pronunciation:

  Near

- Meaning:

  Never

- Example of use:

  "I'll ne'er forget our time together."

Ne'erday

- Pronunciation:

  Near-day

- Meaning:

  New Year's Day

- Example of use:

  "We always have a big meal on Ne'erday."

Nippy

• Pronunciation:

Nip-py

• Meaning:

Cold

• Example of use:

"It's a bit nippy outside, better grab a jacket."

Noo

• Pronunciation:

Noo

• Meaning:

Just Now

• Example of use:

"I'll do it noo, just give me a minute."

Numpty

• Pronunciation:

Nump-tee

• Meaning:

Foolish or Simpleton Person

• Example of use:

"Don't be such a numpty, use your head."

Och!

- Pronunciation:

Och

- Meaning:

Oh! Or Expression of Surprise

- Example of use:

"Och, I can't believe you did that!"

Onding

- Pronunciation:

On-ding

- Meaning:

Continuous Fall of Rain or Snow

- Example of use:

"The onding has been relentless this winter."

Outwith

- Pronunciation:

Out-with

- Meaning:

Outside

- Example of use:

"You'll find the tools outwith the shed."

Ower

- Pronunciation:

Ow-er

- Meaning:

Over

- Example of use:

"The party is ower at midnight."

Oxter

- Pronunciation:

Ox-ter

- Meaning:

Armpit

- Example of use:

"He's carrying his bag under his oxter."

Pairt

- Pronunciation:

Part

- Meaning:

Part

- Example of use:

"You played a big pairt in making this happen."

Palaver

- Pronunciation:

Pal-a-ver

- Meaning:

Fuss

- Example of use:

"Let's not make a palaver about this, it's not a big deal."

Patter

- Pronunciation:

Pat-ter

- Meaning:

Chat

- Example of use:

"She's great patter at parties."

Pech

- Pronunciation:

Pech

- Meaning:

Pant

- Example of use:

"After climbing the hill, I was peching for breath."

Peely Wally

- Pronunciation:

  Peel-ee Wall-ee

- Meaning:

  Pale Faced

- Example of use:

  "She looks a bit peely wally today, maybe she's ill."

Peever

- Pronunciation:

  Pee-ver

- Meaning:

  Hopscotch

- Example of use:

  "Let's play some peever after school."

Piece

- Pronunciation:

  Piece

- Meaning:

  Sandwich

- Example of use:

  "I'll have a ham piece for lunch."

Polis

- Pronunciation:

Polis

- Meaning:

Police

- Example of use:

"The polis are patrolling the streets tonight."

Puggled

- Pronunciation:

Pug-gled

- Meaning:

Fatigued

- Example of use:

"After the long hike, I was completely puggled."

Puir

- Pronunciation:

Poor

- Meaning:

Poor

- Example of use:

"They've been living off puir means for years."

Pure

- Pronunciation:

Pyoor

- Meaning:

Very or Extremely

- Example of use:

"That movie was pure brilliant!"

Quine

- Pronunciation:

Kween

- Meaning:

Girl or Young Woman

- Example of use:

"She's a bonnie quine, isn't she?"

Rammy

- Pronunciation:

Rah-mee

- Meaning:

Fight

- Example of use:

"There was a rammy outside the pub last night."

Roaster

- Pronunciation:

Row-ster

- Meaning:

Describing Someone Behaving Irritatingly

- Example of use:

"He's acting like a total roaster today."

Sair

- Pronunciation:

Sair

- Meaning:

Sore

- Example of use:

"My feet are sair after that long walk."

Sang

- Pronunciation:

Sang

- Meaning:

Song

- Example of use:

"She sang a beautiful sang at the concert."

Scran

- Pronunciation:

Skran

- Meaning:

Food

- Example of use:

"I'm starving, let's grab some scran."

Scratcher

- Pronunciation:

Skra-chur

- Meaning:

Bed

- Example of use:

"I can't wait to hit the scratcher after this long day."

Semmit

- Pronunciation:

Sem-mit

- Meaning:

Vest

- Example of use:

"He wore a white semmit under his shirt."

Shieling

- Pronunciation:

Shee-ling

- Meaning:

Mountain Hut

- Example of use:

"They spent the night in a shieling during their hike."

Shoogly

- Pronunciation:

Shoo-glee

- Meaning:

Shake or Wobble

- Example of use:

"The table is a bit shoogly, be careful with it."

Skelf

- Pronunciation:

Skelf

- Meaning:

Thin Fragment or Splinter

- Example of use:

"I got a skelf stuck in my finger."

Skelly

- Pronunciation:

  Skel-ee

- Meaning:

  Squint

- Example of use:

  "She always skellys when she's trying to read."

Skirl

- Pronunciation:

  Skirl

- Meaning:

  Emit a High-pitched Sound

- Example of use:

  "The bagpipes began to skirl as the parade started."

Skite

- Pronunciation:

  Skite

- Meaning:

  Slip or Slide

- Example of use:

  "I nearly skited on the wet pavement."

Skivvy

- Pronunciation:

Skiv-ee

- Meaning:

Domestic Servant or Maid

- Example of use:

"She worked as a skivvy for a wealthy family."

Sleekit

- Pronunciation:

Slee-kit

- Meaning:

Sly

- Example of use:

"He gave me a sleekit look before he left."

Sma

- Pronunciation:

Sma

- Meaning:

Small

- Example of use:

"It's just a sma scratch, nothing to worry about."

Smirr

- Pronunciation:

    Smir

- Meaning:

    Soft Rain or Misting

- Example of use:

    "We walked in the smirr for hours."

Snell

- Pronunciation:

    Snell

- Meaning:

    Very Cold

- Example of use:

    "The wind is snell today, better bundle up."

Sparra

- Pronunciation:

    Spar-ra

- Meaning:

    Sparrow

- Example of use:

    "The garden is full of sparras in the morning."

Spurtle

• Pronunciation:

Sper-tul

• Meaning:

Wooden Kitchen Tool

• Example of use:

"She used the spurtle to stir the porridge."

Stane

• Pronunciation:

Stayn

• Meaning:

Stone

• Example of use:

"He skipped the stane across the water."

Staun

• Pronunciation:

Stawn

• Meaning:

Stand

• Example of use:

"Could you staun over there for a moment?"

Stoor

- Pronunciation:

Stoor

- Meaning:

Dust

- Example of use:

"The wind blew in and lifted the stoor from the road."

Stooshie

- Pronunciation:

Stoo-shee

- Meaning:

Disruption from a Minor Argument

- Example of use:

"There was a big stooshie over who should pay the bill."

Stowed

- Pronunciation:

Stowed

- Meaning:

Full

- Example of use:

"After the meal, I was stowed."

Stramash

- Pronunciation:

  Stra-mash

- Meaning:

  Uproar or Chaos

- Example of use:

  "The party turned into a stramash after midnight."

Stravaig

- Pronunciation:

  Stra-vayg

- Meaning:

  Roam or Wander

- Example of use:

  "Let's stravaig through the woods this afternoon."

Syboe

- Pronunciation:

  Sai-bow

- Meaning:

  Spring Onion

- Example of use:

  "Could you pass me the syboe for the salad?"

Tassie

- Pronunciation:

Tass-ee

- Meaning:

Cup

- Example of use:

"Pour the tea into the tassie."

Tattie

- Pronunciation:

Tat-tee

- Meaning:

Potato

- Example of use:

"She makes the best tattie scones in town."

Telt

- Pronunciation:

Telt

- Meaning:

Told

- Example of use:

"I telt him not to go there."

Thegither

- Pronunciation:

Theg-ither

- Meaning:

Together

- Example of use:

"Let's work on this thegither."

Thirl

- Pronunciation:

Thurl

- Meaning:

Pierce or Drill

- Example of use:

"The cold wind seemed to thirl right through my coat."

Thole

- Pronunciation:

Thole

- Meaning:

Endure

- Example of use:

"She had to thole the pain until the ambulance arrived."

Thrapple

- Pronunciation:

  Thrap-ul

- Meaning:

  Throat

- Example of use:

  "That fishbone is stuck in my thrapple."

Thrawn

- Pronunciation:

  Thrawn

- Meaning:

  Stubborn or Twisted

- Example of use:

  "He's as thrawn as they come."

Trauchle

- Pronunciation:

  Traw-kul

- Meaning:

  Exhausting Task

- Example of use:

  "Moving all that furniture was a real trauchle."

Trews

- Pronunciation:

Trooz

- Meaning:

Tartan Trousers

- Example of use:

"He wore his best trews to the wedding."

Twa

- Pronunciation:

Twa

- Meaning:

Two

- Example of use:

"I'll have twa slices of cake, please."

Unco

- Pronunciation:

Un-co

- Meaning:

Strange or Weird

- Example of use:

"That's an unco tale you're telling."

Verra

- Pronunciation:

Ver-ra

- Meaning:

Very

- Example of use:

"It's verra cold out today."

Wabbit

- Pronunciation:

Wab-it

- Meaning:

Exhausted

- Example of use:

"After the marathon, I was completely wabbit."

Wain

- Pronunciation:

Wayn

- Meaning:

Child

- Example of use:

"Look at the wee wain playing in the garden."

Wan

- Pronunciation:

  Wan

- Meaning:

  One

- Example of use:

  "I'll have wan ticket for the show, please."

Wean

- Pronunciation:

  Ween

- Meaning:

  Children

- Example of use:

  "The park was filled with weans playing on the swings."

Wee Bairn

- Pronunciation:

  Wee Bairn

- Meaning:

  Small Child

- Example of use:

  "The wee bairn toddled around the room, giggling."

Wee

- Pronunciation:

  Wee

- Meaning:

  ## Small or Tiny

- Example of use:

  "She carried a wee bag with her wherever she went."

Weel-kent

- Pronunciation:

  Weel-kent

- Meaning:

  ## Well-known or Renowned

- Example of use:

  "The pub is a weel-kent spot for locals and tourists alike."

Wersh

- Pronunciation:

  Wersh

- Meaning:

  ## Tasteless or Unpalatable

- Example of use:

  "The soup was so wersh, I couldn't finish it."

Whaur

- Pronunciation:

  Whar

- Meaning:

  Where

- Example of use:

  "Whaur did ye leave the keys?"

Wheech

- Pronunciation:

  Weech

- Meaning:

  Move Quickly or Suddenly

- Example of use:

  "The cat wheeched across the room chasing a mouse."

Widd

- Pronunciation:

  Wid

- Meaning:

  Wood

- Example of use:

  "He carved a beautiful sculpture out of a block of widd."

Windae

· Pronunciation:

Win-dae

· Meaning:

Windows

· Example of use:

"She opened the windae to let in some fresh air."

Wrang

· Pronunciation:

Wrang

· Meaning:

Wrong or Mistake

· Example of use:

"I ken I was wrang, and I'm sorry."

Ye

· Pronunciation:

Yee

· Meaning:

You

· Example of use:

"Ye should have seen the look on her face."

Yer

- Pronunciation:

  Yer

- Meaning:

  Your

- Example of use:

  "Is that yer jacket on the chair?"

Yett

- Pronunciation:

  Yet

- Meaning:

  Gate

- Example of use:

  "The sheep were gathered near the yett waiting to be let in."

Yin

- Pronunciation:

  Yin

- Meaning:

  One

- Example of use:

  "Can I have yin more slice of cake, please?"

A bawhair away

•Meaning:

When a Scotsman mentions being "a bawhair away," they actually mean just how close something really is. So, if one of the locals informs you that the finishing line is "a bawhair away," the victory may be nearer than you thought.

•Scotland Phrase:

Ah Dinnae Ken

•Meaning:

This actually is the Scottish way of saying that one doesn't know-when one is faced with a moment of doubt or a lack of knowledge. So, the next time you're sitting around and contemplating all life's imponderables, just shrug your shoulders and say with pride, "Ah Dinnae Ken."

•Scotland Phrase:

Away an Bile Yer Heid!

•Meaning:

"Away an Bile Yer Heid!" is a lively Scottish phrase instructing someone to go away or leave you be. So when those annoying distractions come knocking, make sure to hold this up like a shield and give yourself some room.

•Scotland Phrase:

Aye cheers

•Meaning:

If a Scot says, "Aye cheers," then he is thanking you but in a sarcastic manner. So when someone hands you over a cup of tea that has gone cold and you return with an indifferent "Aye cheers," then you are politely acknowledging the act with an underbelly of irony.

- Scotland Phrase:

Aye right

- Meaning:

This is a Scottish way of saying, "Right." This is a skeptic's, and disbelieving, word/phrase. So, whenever one hears a story that has to be too good to be true, respond with a ready "Aye right."

- Scotland Phrase:

Aye so he will

- Meaning:

This is Scots for "Yes, he will," but it really means "I doubt he will." That is to say, if a Scot says, "Aye so he will," he's doubting whether the person in question can or will do something. So, the next time you feel doubtful about the outcome of some pending event, simply nod knowingly and murmur, "Aye so he will."

- Scotland Phrase:

Aye, aye okay

- Meaning:

This "Aye, aye okay" is a gentle way of saying yes when accepting with displeasure. So next time you find yourself in any situation and are not exactly pleased about it, just say, "Aye, aye okay."

- Scotland Phrase:

Bide yer wheesht !!

- Meaning:

"Bide yer wheesht !! " Is means shut up or keep quiet. It is an instruction given to someone to keep quiet or shut up.

Check oot that big feartie

•Meaning:

Tease a timid friend in a playful way, pointing at his fear with a smile
to lighten up his moment of nervousness.

Dinna fash yersel

•Meaning:

When troubles weigh you down, let this remind you to keep your head above
the turmoil and remain calm in the eye of the storm of emotions.

Don't gie's yer pish

•Meaning:

Cut through nonsensical chatter, allowable when trying to redirect conversations
toward meaningful exchanges.

D'ye cause a right stooshie

•Meaning:

Defuse conflicts by signaling a retreat from unnecessary commotion,
avoiding unnecessary drama.

D'ye go aff yer nut

• Meaning:

This phrase keeps you calm during emotional situations;
it calls for restraint and calm.

• Scotland Phrase:

D'ye huv a blether

• Meaning:

Encourage people to be more succinct with their communication by giving a nudge
toward brevity in conversations; keep the dialogues engaging.

• Scotland Phrase:

Gie it laldy

• Meaning:

Give your all in every endeavor with this rallying cry that will launch you
into greatness.

• Scotland Phrase:

Haud yer wheesht

• Meaning:

Ask for silence in loud areas so that calm may be brought into a sea of chatter.

- Scotland Phrase:

Haw you

- Meaning:

This is one of the ways to politely command attention to start talking nicely in some social gathering.

- Scotland Phrase:

Ah must admit, ah shat masel a wee bit

- Meaning:

Show a wee, honest-to-goodness worry or concern with this honest admission and bridge gaps in uncertainty.

- Scotland Phrase:

In the Nick of Time

- Meaning:

Congratulate timely interventions and victorious moments at the last minute with this phrase, adding an element of excitement to it.

- Scotland Phrase:

It's a Dreich Day

- Meaning:

Describe horrible weather with this phrase, embracing the poetic charm of Scottish expression in your observations.

• Scotland Phrase:

I'm gonnae shoot the craw

• Meaning:

Playfully signal your departure using this phrase; add humor
to the parting moments.

• Scotland Phrase:

Keep the heid

• Meaning:

Keep cool and calm when events seem to be getting out of hand.

• Scotland Phrase:

Ma Heid's Mince!

• Meaning:

Feeling confused or disorientated about something.

• Scotland Phrase:

Ma heid's up ma arse the day

• Meaning:

When you are not right, not quite yourself.

- Scotland Phrase:

Och, yer a long time deid

- Meaning:

Make the most of life, for you will be dead a long time.

- Scotland Phrase:

We've been up, doon an' roon the hooses

- Meaning:

Have searched or exploring everywhere.

- Scotland Phrase:

Whit's fur ye'll no go by ye

- Meaning:

What will be, will be, as it were said - an appeal to fate or destiny.

- Scotland Phrase:

What's wrang wi the glaikit coupon?

- Meaning:

Tease them as looking puzzled or confused.

• Scotland Phrase:

Ye ken fine whit's goin on

• Meaning:

Suggest one has a complete understanding of what is happening.

• Scotland Phrase:

Yer a bawhair away

• Meaning:

Tell someone they are not very near to it, with the implication of some small distance or difference.

• Scotland Phrase:

Yer a total numpty

• Meaning:

Playfully tease someone that they are not acting sensibly or smartly .

• Scotland Phrase:

Yer Aff Yer Heid

• Meaning:

Tell someone they are acting crazy, or out of their mind.